The Beignet That Almost Got Away

By Joanne Mehrtens and Pat Roig

For Bruce, Meghann and Kayleigh
- J.M.

For Ken, Stef, Kelly and Greg
-Keep dreaming!
- P.R.

No part of this publication may be reproduced in whole or in part, or stored in a retrieval system, or transmitted in any form or by any means, electronic, mechanical, photocopying, recording or otherwise, without written permission of the publisher.
For information regarding permission, write to:
P&J's Creative Days
P.O. Box 55607
Metairie, LA 70055-5607.

ISBN 1-4243-0881-X

Text copyright © 2009 by Joanne Mehrtens and Pat Roig
Illustrations copyright © by Joanne Mehrtens
All rights reserved. Printed in the U.S.A.

Book layout and design by Rebecca Pitre

Website design by Tina Lagarde

Visit our website:
www.theadventuresofralphandroxanne.com

Contact us at:
info@pandjdays.com

Printed by **MPRESS**
4100 Howard Ave.
New Orleans, LA 70125
www.mpressnow.com

Mississippi River

Down in Louisiana,
in the city that care forgot

lived two cockroaches
that loved food a lot!

New Orleans is a city
known for fine cuisine

but for Ralph and Roxanne
times were really lean.

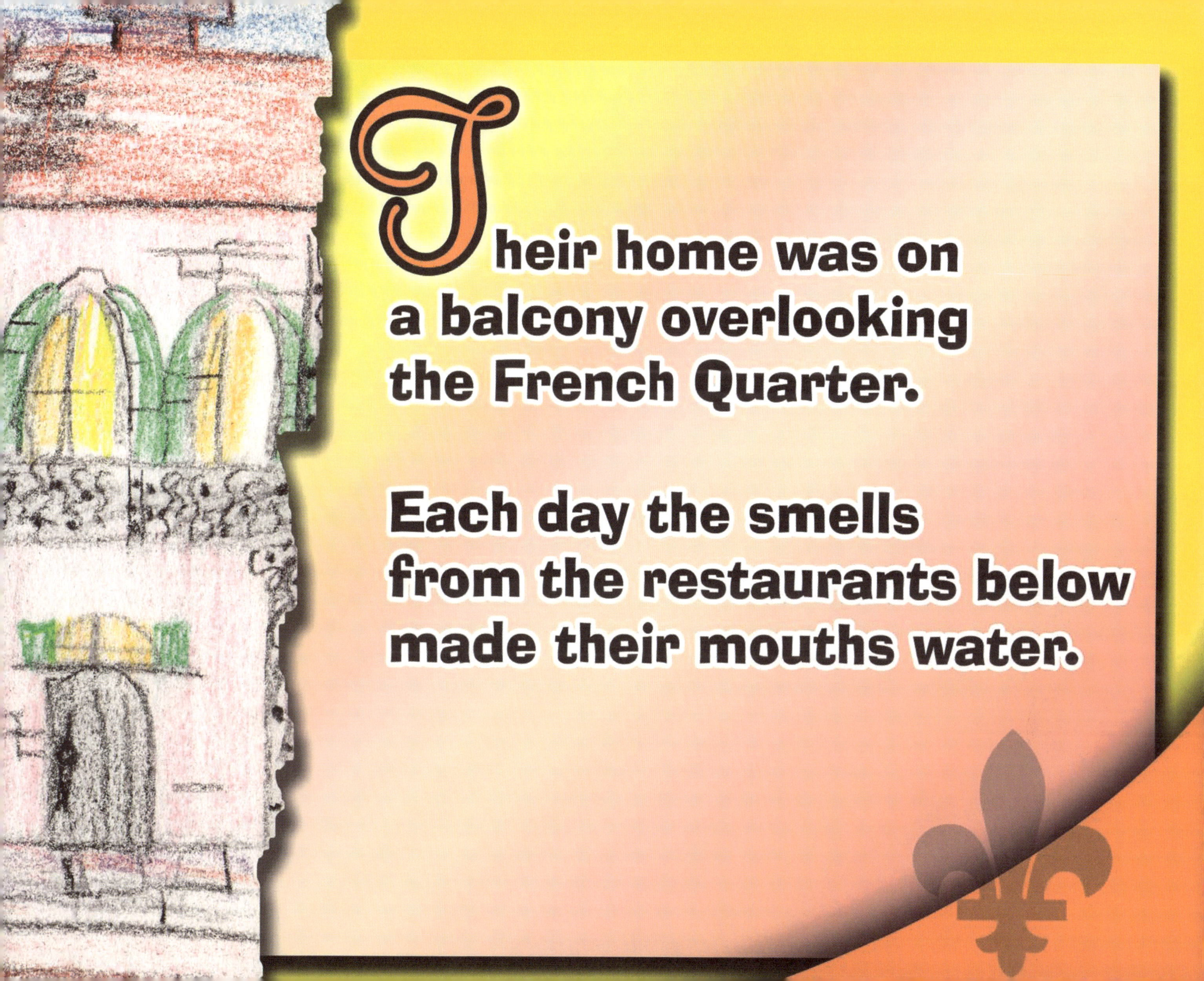

Their home was on a balcony overlooking the French Quarter.

Each day the smells from the restaurants below made their mouths water.

One smell in particular made their stomachs respond

the scent of crispy beignets from Café Du Monde.

CAFÉ DU MONDE

Amidst the clatter of cups and the shuffle of feet

these intrepid insects were beckoned by the powdered sugar so sweet.

And there on a plate,
crispy and steamy it lay

the object of their craving
one lone beignet.

Ralph and Roxanne gave each other looks of fierce determination.

This beignet would be theirs if they formed a collaboration.

Just as they reached
the point
of their desire,

a hand came down and
raised the beignet higher.

In a paper sack
the sweet snack resided

"Don't let that beignet get away!"
screamed Roxanne excited.

Natche

They kept that bag in their sights as it headed to the river.

The music from the Natchez steamboat made their antennae quiver.

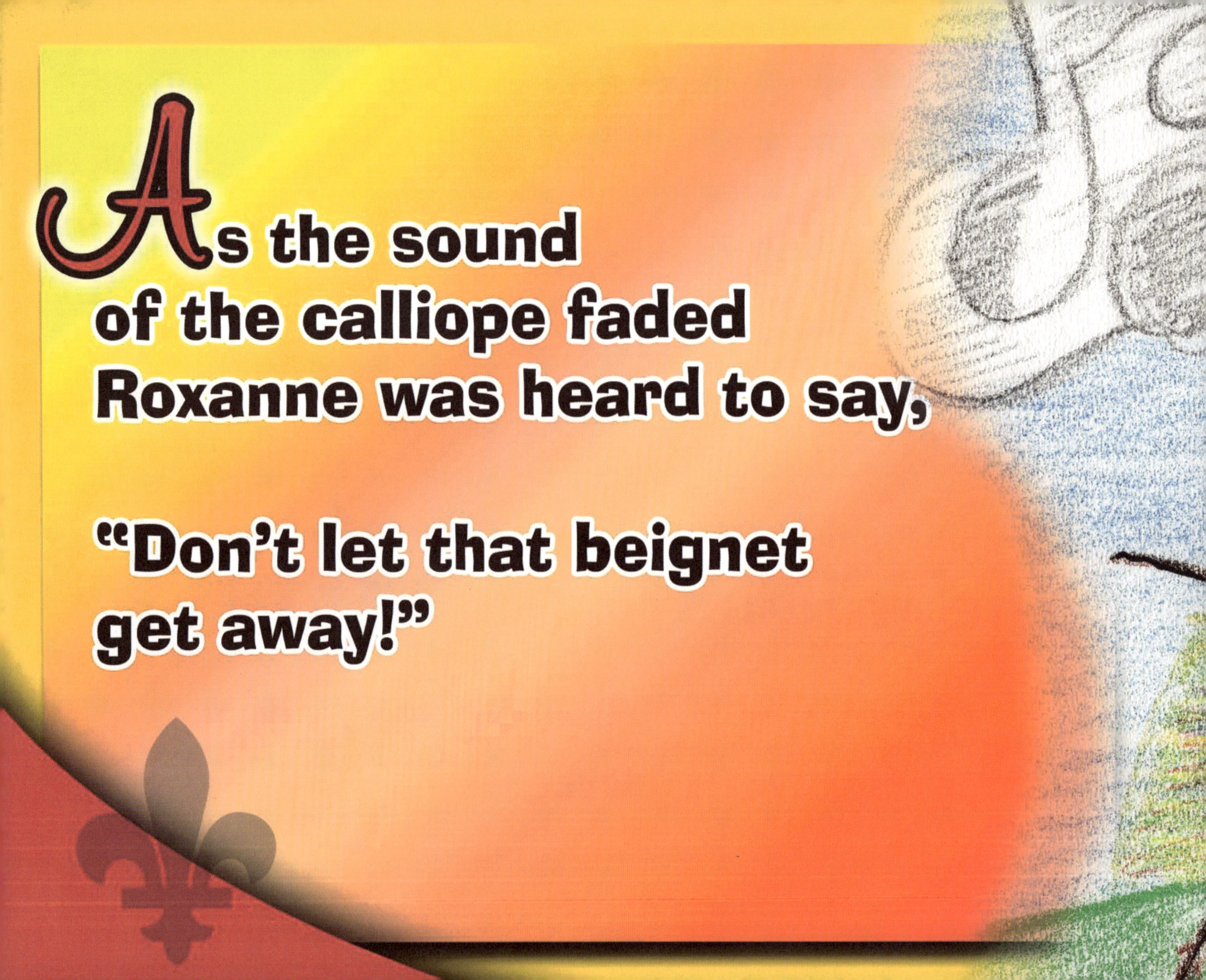

As the sound
of the calliope faded
Roxanne was heard to say,

"Don't let that beignet
get away!"

ANDREW JACKSON

Suddenly the bag took
a turn to Jackson Square

a place where art abounds
and music fills the air.

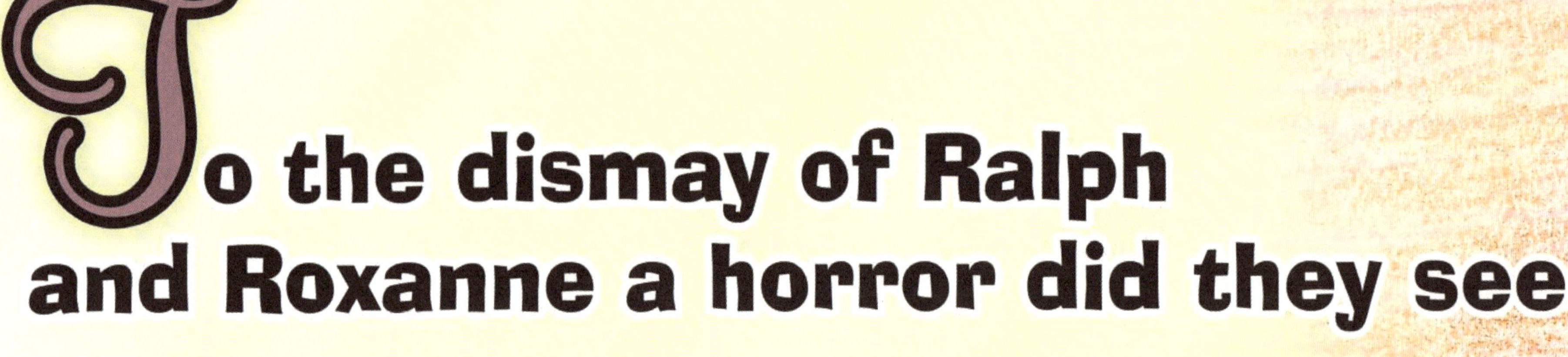

To the dismay of Ralph
and Roxanne a horror did they see

the pigeons were being fed
their beignet for free.

"Don't let that beignet get away!"

The clip clop of hooves and
the rolling of wooden wheels

led the bag to a horse drawn carriage
as Roxanne let out a squeal,

"Don't let that beignet get away!"

As Ralph and Roxanne followed the bag into Jackson Square

they stopped by a crowd watching a mime performing there.

Ralph and Roxanne stared at their bag with trepidation

as a hand set it aside to reach for a balloon creation.

Ralph and Roxanne exchanged looks of jubilation

the beignet was theirs
now they'll feast
with **EXALTATION!**

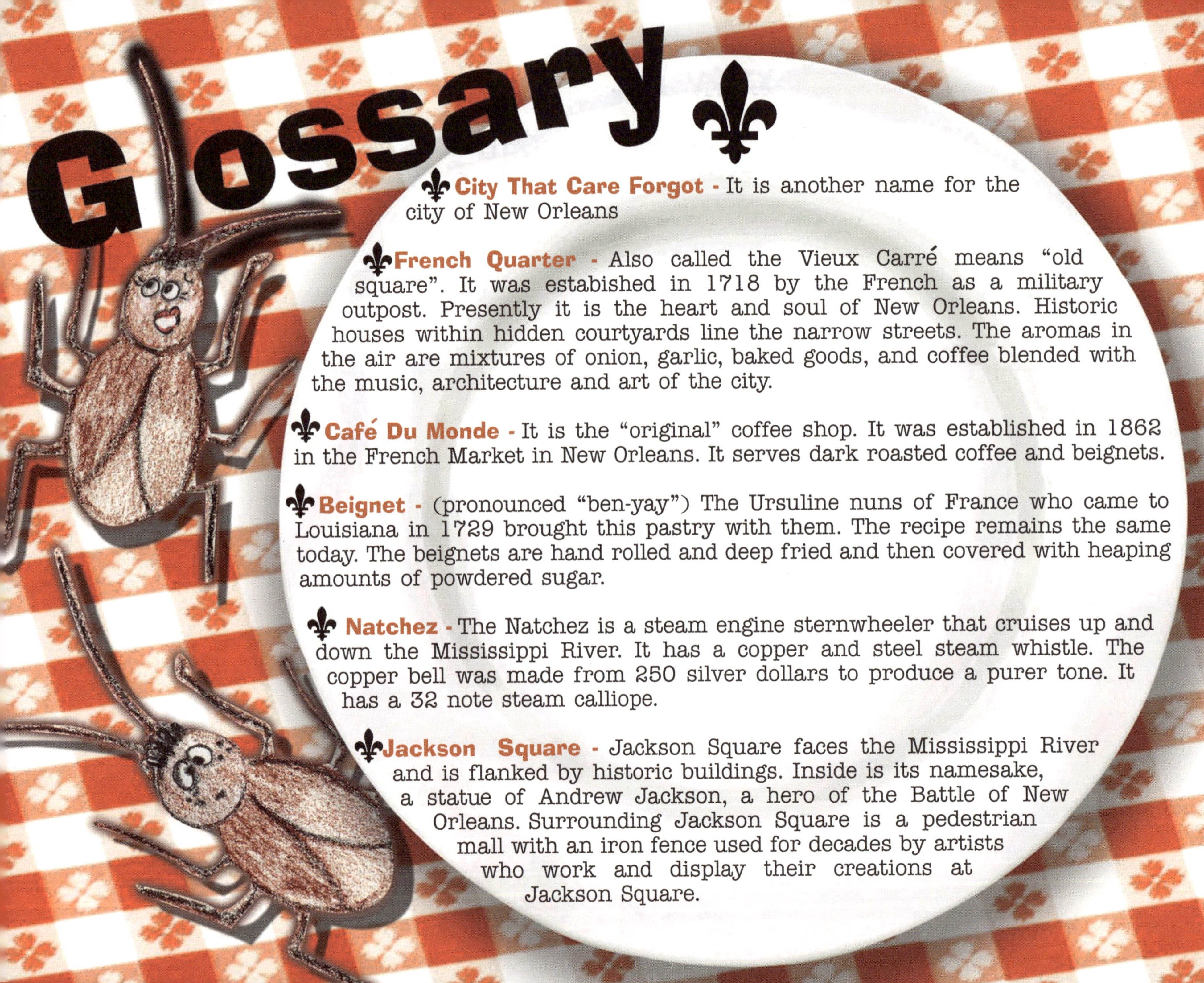

Glossary

City That Care Forgot - It is another name for the city of New Orleans

French Quarter - Also called the Vieux Carré means "old square". It was estabished in 1718 by the French as a military outpost. Presently it is the heart and soul of New Orleans. Historic houses within hidden courtyards line the narrow streets. The aromas in the air are mixtures of onion, garlic, baked goods, and coffee blended with the music, architecture and art of the city.

Café Du Monde - It is the "original" coffee shop. It was established in 1862 in the French Market in New Orleans. It serves dark roasted coffee and beignets.

Beignet - (pronounced "ben-yay") The Ursuline nuns of France who came to Louisiana in 1729 brought this pastry with them. The recipe remains the same today. The beignets are hand rolled and deep fried and then covered with heaping amounts of powdered sugar.

Natchez - The Natchez is a steam engine sternwheeler that cruises up and down the Mississippi River. It has a copper and steel steam whistle. The copper bell was made from 250 silver dollars to produce a purer tone. It has a 32 note steam calliope.

Jackson Square - Jackson Square faces the Mississippi River and is flanked by historic buildings. Inside is its namesake, a statue of Andrew Jackson, a hero of the Battle of New Orleans. Surrounding Jackson Square is a pedestrian mall with an iron fence used for decades by artists who work and display their creations at Jackson Square.

P & J's CREATIVE DAYS, LLC

P.O. Box 55607 • Metairie, Louisiana 70055-5607

Please send me______ copies of **The Beignet That Almost Got Away**
at $12.95 per copy (Price includes postage and handling.)

Please send me______ copies of **Counting Around the Neutral Ground**
at $12.95 per copy (Price includes postage and handling.)

Enclosed is my check or money order for $______________

Name____

Address______________________________

City______________________________State________Zip______

Please allow 10-12 business days for delivery

Other titles available by Joanne Mehrtens and Pat Roig